Original title:
Twilight Tails and Dreamy Trails

Copyright © 2024 Creative Arts Management OÜ
All rights reserved.

Author: Amelia Montgomery
ISBN HARDBACK: 978-9916-90-528-9
ISBN PAPERBACK: 978-9916-90-529-6

Nighttime's Silent Symphony

The stars awake in velvet skies,
Whispers drift where moonlight lies.
In shadows deep, the soft winds sing,
A lullaby that night will bring.

Crickets chirp in tender tune,
While fireflies dance beneath the moon.
Each note a breath, each sigh a sound,
In nighttime's arms, peace can be found.

Footprints in the Indigo Dust

Along the path where dreams do roam,
I leave my mark, I find my home.
Indigo dust beneath my feet,
A journey born from rhythmic beat.

With every step, the world unfolds,
Stories whispered, secrets told.
In twilight's hue, I trace the way,
Footprints left, come what may.

Glimmers of Twilight's Kiss

In the hush of dusk, colors blend,
A soft embrace as night descends.
Golden rays meet purple skies,
Glimmers of hope in firefly sighs.

As daylight fades, dreams take flight,
Bathed in the glow of coming night.
Each moment shared, a treasure to keep,
In twilight's arms, the heart finds peace.

The Journey into the Unknown

Beyond the hills where shadows play,
A road untraveled calls my way.
With every step, new tales unfold,
A story waiting to be told.

Fear dances close, but courage stays,
Lighting the path through winding ways.
In the heart of night, with stars to guide,
I take the leap, embrace the tide.

Ethereal Whispers of Dusk

In twilight's gentle breath we sigh,
The fading light, a soft goodbye.
With colors blend in whispered grace,
The stars awake, the night's embrace.

As shadows deep begin to weave,
A tapestry that we believe.
Each moment holds a sacred dream,
In dusk's embrace, we softly gleam.

Veils of Starlight and Secrets

Through veils of starlight, whispers breathe,
Secrets linger, softly wreathed.
In silken night, the world awakes,
With every glance, the silence breaks.

The moonlight dances on your skin,
Inviting magic to begin.
With every heartbeat, stories rise,
Where hopes reside beneath the skies.

Nightfall's Gentle Embrace

Nightfall wraps the weary land,
In tender arms, a soft command.
The world retreats, a hush prevails,
While starlit dreams begin their trails.

Each breath draws in the calm of night,
As shadows weave their starry light.
With open hearts, we find our place,
In nightfall's gentle, warm embrace.

Shadows Dance on the Horizon

As shadows dance on the horizon,
The daylight fades, a sweet diversion.
With every step, the night unfolds,
In silver tones and stories told.

The whispers linger, soft and clear,
Every moment draws us near.
In twilight's charm, our spirits rise,
As darkness blooms beneath the skies.

Wandering Through Umbral Gardens

In shadows deep, where whispers play,
The moonlight dances, soft and gray.
Petals fall like dreams untold,
In umbral gardens, secrets unfold.

The scent of night fills the air,
Each breath a story, rich and rare.
Through twisted paths, I lose my way,
In this wild realm, I long to stay.

Beneath the stars, a ghostly glow,
Awakens feelings buried low.
With every step, the silence sighs,
A symphony of quiet cries.

Here time drifts by, a gentle thief,
In every moment, hidden grief.
Yet in this maze, I find my heart,
In umbral gardens, I'll never part.

Dreams at the Edge of Night

In whispers soft, the dreams take flight,
Woven threads in the edge of night.
Stars twinkle like eyes that watch,
As the world drifts in a gentle swatch.

The moon, a lantern, guides the way,
Through shadows where the lost hearts play.
Silken thoughts on a breeze do drift,
Carried softly, a nighttime gift.

Each lingering echo, a story spun,
Of battles lost and victories won.
In these dreams, we find our truth,
Recalling lost loves of our youth.

At the cusp where visions dwell,
A timeless spell, a whispered tell.
With every sigh, the darkness weaves,
The sweetest tales our heart believes.

Where the Light Meets the Dark

In a dance of twilight, shadows blend,
Where light soft kisses night's dark end.
Faint silhouettes begin to stir,
As day gives way, and dreams confer.

Golden rays entwine with gray,
In this moment, night holds sway.
A fragile peace fills the air,
Where whispers linger, secrets bare.

The stars emerge, brave and bold,
Guardians of stories yet untold.
Across the sky, a canvas wide,
Where hopes and fears run side by side.

In that space, we learn to breathe,
In light, in dark, we find reprieve.
A balance struck, a heart's refrain,
Where joy and sorrow meet again.

Embrace of the Coming Night

As dusk descends, the world grows still,
The gentle night wraps like a quilt.
A lullaby hums through the trees,
Carried softly by a tender breeze.

The sun retreats, its colors fade,
In twilight's glow, the dreams are made.
A canvas painted in shades of blue,
Where everything feels fresh and new.

Embrace the night, let worries cease,
In its arms, we find our peace.
With every star, a wish takes flight,
As we surrender to the night.

In whispered moments, hearts do mend,
As shadows lengthen, friendships blend.
Together under this starlit dome,
In the embrace of night, we are home.

The Last Glow of Day

The sun dips low, a fireball bright,
Its golden rays fade into night.
Whispers of dusk, a soft embrace,
Nature bows down, in timeless grace.

Clouds painted pink, a canvas wide,
As shadows stretch, and stars collide.
The world sighs deep, a tranquil air,
In twilight's hush, all worries bare.

Enchanted Paths Beneath the Stars

Starlit trails call out to me,
Where dreams and wishes dance so free.
Under the moon's gentle gaze,
Magic whispers in hidden ways.

Each step I take, the night unfolds,
Stories of wonders yet untold.
With every breath, the cosmos sings,
Inviting me to dream on wings.

Evening's Serenade

The nightingale sings a tender tune,
Beneath the watchful silver moon.
With every note, the night renews,
A symphony of soft, sweet blues.

The breeze carries secrets of the night,
As shadows gather, out of sight.
In evening's arms, the world finds peace,
A quiet moment, a sweet release.

The Gentle Fade of Daylight

Daylight wanes with a soft farewell,
As twilight weaves its magic spell.
Colors mingle, a painter's dream,
In fading light, the stars will gleam.

The horizon blushes, kissed by dusk,
In silence wrapped, the world finds trust.
With gentle whispers, night will hold,
The fading tales of days of old.

Journeys into the Gentle Abyss

In shadows deep where whispers dwell,
A current strong begins to swell.
With every breath, the silence sings,
And pulls me close to hidden things.

Visions dance, both near and far,
Guided softly by the stars.
Each step I take, a tale unfolds,
In the gentle abyss, courage holds.

Beneath the waves of dreams I swim,
Through twilight realms that ebb and brim.
The heartbeats pulse, a sacred thread,
In this quiet place, I am led.

Awake in stillness, fears release,
In the deep, I find my peace.
A journey rich in hues divine,
The gentle abyss, forever mine.

The Allure of the Crescent Veil

A crescent moon with silver light,
Whispers secrets in the night.
Veils of mist, they slowly creep,
Embracing dreams while the world sleeps.

Stars entwined in velvet skies,
Draw us close with ancient sighs.
In this glow, we drift and sway,
The crescent veil will guide our way.

Through shadows, soft as whispered prayer,
Promises linger in the air.
Each moment wrapped in twilight's tease,
The allure beckons with gentle ease.

Lost in wonder, time will bend,
As the night begins to blend.
With every breath, we intertwine,
Beneath the crescent, love will shine.

Whispers of the Dusk

As daylight fades and shadows play,
The whispers of the dusk hold sway.
Colors melt into a soft embrace,
In twilight's arms, we find our place.

Crickets chirp their serenade,
While memories in silence wade.
The air is thick with stories told,
Of dreams departed, yet to unfold.

Each flicker of the firelight,
Invokes the magic of the night.
In gentle breezes, secrets sway,
Whispers linger, guiding our way.

With every heartbeat, moments pass,
Through dusk's embrace, we find our glass.
Reflections dance on fading day,
In whispers of dusk, we drift away.

Secrets of the Starlit Path

Beneath the map of endless skies,
Secrets shimmer, softly rise.
The starlit path, a journey's grace,
Leads us to a sacred place.

Footsteps light on ancient ground,
In every shadow, wisdom found.
Galaxies gaze with knowing eyes,
As we wander under sighs.

Each twinkle tells a tale of old,
Of dreams pursued and hearts that bold.
With every step, the night unfolds,
The secrets in the stars are told.

Hand in hand, we trace the light,
Through cosmic waves that feel so right.
In the silence, truth imparts,
The starlit path ignites our hearts.

Fading Footprints on a Dreamy Lane

Footprints softly vanish, beneath whispering trees,
Memories of laughter carried by the breeze.
Sunset spills gold on the winding trail,
Dreams like shadows in this quiet vale.

Once vibrant steps now barely trace,
As twilight descends, time begins to race.
A path of wonder, where dreams intertwine,
Fading footprints linger, as we redefine.

Starlight's Gentle Embrace

Underneath the vast sky, starlight gleams,
Whispering soft secrets, cradling our dreams.
Each twinkle a promise, joyous and bright,
Guiding our hearts through the infinite night.

Embers of hope dance in the dark,
A celestial story written in spark.
Wrapped in the cosmic, a serene embrace,
We find our solace in this timeless space.

The Canvas of Evening

Brushstrokes of twilight on a canvas so wide,
Colors of dusk where the day must abide.
A palette of dreams, painted in sighs,
As stars come alive in the night's gentle rise.

Crimson gives way to the indigo hue,
Each moment a masterpiece, fresh and anew.
The horizon softly whispers tales untold,
In the canvas of evening, our hearts unfold.

Following the Ethereal Path

Through the misty woods, an ethereal trail,
Where whispers of magic in the air sail.
Each step a journey, each breath a chance,
To follow the dreams in a starry dance.

Moonlight beckons us to take flight,
Through shadows and dreams, into the night.
Hand in hand we wander, hearts open wide,
Following the path where the spirits guide.

Shadows on the Horizon

Dark clouds gather, whispers loom,
A twilight blush dispels the gloom.
Footsteps falter on the shore,
As shadows stretch, we seek for more.

The sea reflects the fading light,
Waves of whispers, dreams take flight.
In the distance, stars ignite,
Promise of the coming night.

Lanterns in the Gloaming

Softly glowing, lanterns sway,
Guiding hearts on twilight's way.
Flickering hopes in dusky skies,
Where secrets hide and silence lies.

Breezes carry songs of old,
Tales of love and legends told.
In the gloam, we find our peace,
As dusk embraces night's release.

Serene Strolls at Sundown

Strolling gently, hand in hand,
Footprints kissed by golden sand.
The horizon blushes, a tender sight,
As day surrenders to the night.

Whispers of the evening breeze,
Rustling leaves in gentle tease.
Moments linger, softly bound,
In the calm of sundown found.

Echoes of Evening

The darkness hums a lullaby,
As stars blink softly in the sky.
Echoes dance through shadowed trees,
Whispers carried by the breeze.

A fleeting moment, pure and rare,
Night weaves magic through the air.
With every heartbeat, time stands still,
In the hush, all souls will fill.

Mystic Wanderings at Day's End

The sun dips low, the sky ablaze,
Whispers of twilight in a soft haze.
Shadows stretch long across the glade,
Mystic paths through the dusk parade.

Footsteps echo on the forest floor,
Where secrets hide and legends soar.
Stars blink awake in the velvet deep,
Through dreams and silence, wanderers creep.

Reflections in the Evening Mist

Gentle fog embraces the fading light,
Mirrors of memory in the still of night.
The world dissolves in a silver veil,
As scents of earth ride the evening's trail.

Rippling waters hold the sky's glow,
Each ripple tells tales of long ago.
Softly the echoes of twilight sing,
Inviting the heart to feel the spring.

The Fable of the Fading Sun

Once there was a sun so bold,
A light that danced, a warmth to hold.
But time weaves tales that shadows spin,
As dusk approaches, the day grows thin.

In its descent, it whispers low,
Of dreams and wishes, of seeds to sow.
Fables spoken in colors bright,
With every sunset comes the night.

Glistening Embers of the Night

Moonlight spills like a silver stream,
Casting sparkles where the shadows gleam.
In the quiet hum of the starry dome,
Glistening embers start to roam.

A fire crackles in the gentle breeze,
As night unfolds its mysteries.
Stories whispered of love and lore,
In the night's embrace, forevermore.

Celestial Paths and Gossamer Dreams

Beneath the stars, whispers unfold,
A tapestry of stories untold.
Winding through the night's gentle breath,
Gossamer dreams, in twilight's depth.

Silver beams dance on the silent sea,
Guiding hearts where they long to be.
In the vastness, horizons gleam,
Celestial paths weave a delicate dream.

Fable of the Setting Sun

When shadows stretch and colors blend,
The day whispers softly, 'This is the end.'
A fable spun with hues of gold,
In every sunset, a story told.

As twilight paints the world anew,
The horizon blushes with a pinkish hue.
Stars awaken in the velvet sky,
Time dances gently, as moments fly.

Treading Softly on Starry Trails

Through the night, our dreams take flight,
Treading softly, hearts alight.
Beneath a sky of endless schemes,
We wander freely in woven dreams.

In the stillness, secrets hum,
A lullaby of night has come.
Stars align with every sigh,
Lighting paths where wishes lie.

The Magic of the Coming Dusk

In the hush before the night takes hold,
Magic whispers, sweet and bold.
Crickets chirp in rhythmic grace,
As twilight wraps the world in lace.

With every shade of deepening blue,
The magic stirs, reborn anew.
In the dusk's embrace, we find our way,
Where dreams awaken and hopes sway.

The Dance of Shadows and Dreams

In twilight's grasp, shadows sway,
Their whispers soft, night blends with day.
Dreams take flight on silver beams,
Dancing lightly, woven streams.

Clouds pass by like fleeting thoughts,
In the silence, the heartbeat's caught.
A world where hope and fear unite,
In this dance of dark and light.

Beneath the stars, secrets unfold,
Stories waiting to be told.
Echoes linger in the breeze,
As shadows whisper through the trees.

Together they weave a timeless thread,
In a realm where senses tread.
A gentle sigh, a soulful plea,
As shadows dance, forever free.

Harmonies of Nightfall

As daylight fades, the night begins,
Soft melodies play, the darkness wins.
Stars twinkle bright in the velvet sky,
Their silver notes like lullabies.

Moonlit paths, serene and calm,
Embrace the soul like a tender balm.
Crickets chirp a rhythmic tune,
Under the watchful eye of the moon.

Whispers of winds through rustling leaves,
Crafting tales that the heart believes.
Each note dances through shadowed glades,
In harmonies where silence pervades.

In the stillness, the world unwinds,
In night's embrace, solace finds.
A symphony of dreams takes flight,
In the beautiful depths of night.

Roads of Lost Whispers

Footsteps echo on the cobblestone,
Where forgotten dreams have often grown.
Winds carry secrets like fading sighs,
On roads where lost time softly lies.

Each corner turned, a memory calls,
In twilight's glow, the soft light falls.
A journey woven through the years,
With laughter, sorrow, hopes, and tears.

Gathered whispers in the night,
Guide the seekers toward the light.
Silent stories left untold,
In the embrace of time so bold.

Paths diverge where shadows meet,
In every heart, a bittersweet.
For every road, a tale to share,
On the winds of dreams that lay bare.

Beneath the Sapphire Skies

Beneath the dome of sapphire blue,
Where clouds drift lightly, calm and true.
The sun spills gold on fields of green,
In a canvas where joy is seen.

Birds take flight on gentle air,
Their songs are sweet, a lover's prayer.
With every note, the world ignites,
Beneath the canvas of endless nights.

The rivers flow like whispered dreams,
Reflecting light in playful beams.
Nature's lullaby softly hums,
In harmony, the beauty comes.

Under the vast, embracing throng,
Life finds rhythm, strong and long.
In this space where hearts unite,
Beneath the sapphire sky so bright.

Dancing Shadows in the Night

Under a silver moon's glow,
Whispers of the wind flow.
Figures move, soft and light,
Dancing shadows in the night.

Footprints trace in the dark,
Each step a fleeting spark.
Echoes drift on velvet air,
Stars above, a silent prayer.

In the stillness, hearts collide,
Find a rhythm, deep inside.
Embers glow, a soft embrace,
Lost within this sacred space.

In shadows, dreams take flight,
Guided by the pale moonlight.
A dance where spirits sing,
In the night, our souls take wing.

Echoes Beneath the Celestial Dome

Underneath the vast expanse,
Stars twinkle in their dance.
Whispers float through silent air,
Echoes beneath the celestial dome.

Galaxies spin in the night,
Painting wonders, sheer delight.
Each twinkle tells a tale,
Of timeless dreams that sail.

Soft moons cradle ancient lore,
Secrets held on cosmic shore.
In the dark, we find our place,
Amidst the stars, we trace.

Thoughts reach out through endless skies,
In the silence, truth belies.
Together, we shall roam,
In the echoes, find our home.

Twilight Mirages and Dreamscapes

As daylight fades to twilight hue,
The world transforms, a magic view.
Mirages dance on golden beams,
In twilight's grasp, we weave our dreams.

Clouds drift like thoughts in the breeze,
Painting stories with such ease.
Every color, a brush of fate,
In dreamscapes where we contemplate.

Horizon whispers secrets old,
In its arms, we are consoled.
The night extends a gentle hand,
Together in this timeless land.

With each moment, shadows play,
In twilight's glow, we find our way.
A journey through the fading light,
Into the arms of the night.

The Brush of Dusk's Hand

When the sun dips low and dim,
Dusk begins its quiet hymn.
A painter with a gentle sweep,
The brush of dusk brings dreams to keep.

Hues of orange melt to gray,
As light and shadow dance and sway.
The world, a canvas, touched anew,
In dusk's embrace, all feels true.

Crescent moons begin to rise,
Draped in starlight, nature sighs.
Softly, whispers weave the night,
Carried forth on twilight's flight.

Each brushstroke tells a tale untold,
Of secret journeys, brave and bold.
In dusk's calm, our hearts expand,
Together bound by dusk's gentle hand.

Murmurs from the Edge of Night

Whispers drift in twilight set,
Shadows dance, a soft vignette.
Stars awaken, pairs unite,
Fleeting glimmers of delight.

Gentle breezes, secrets told,
Moonlight gleams, a thread of gold.
In the stillness, hearts align,
Murmurs linger, sweet and fine.

Night unfolds its velvet shroud,
Crickets sing, a quiet crowd.
In the dark, dreams take their flight,
Murmurs echo, pure and bright.

With the dawn, the magic wane,
Yet the whispers still remain.
Memory of that soothing night,
Holds us close till morning light.

A Spectrum of Dreams Unfurled

Colors blend in dusk's embrace,
Fleeting shadows, softening space.
Wishes weave on silken threads,
In the mind where nothing dreads.

Opalescent visions soar,
Through the folds, we dream for more.
Twinkling thoughts in vibrant hues,
Awake the heart, ignite the muse.

Each dream a tale, an echo bright,
Linking souls in shared twilight.
With the dawn, their whispers fade,
Yet in our hearts, they're never laid.

Spectrum holds the night's allure,
Every dream, a path so pure.
Though the world may pull apart,
Together still, we share one heart.

Luminescent Dreams in Fading Light

Glimmers bright in evening's glow,
Touching hearts we deeply know.
Stories rise amidst the haze,
Lightly drifting in the maze.

Fading rays of golden sun,
Whisper softly, day is done.
In the twilight, dreams ignite,
Luminescent, pure delight.

Every thought, a spark divine,
Guiding us on pathways fine.
In the twilight's soft embrace,
Find the warmth in every space.

Though the light may start to wane,
In our dreams, there is no pain.
Hold the magic, let it stay,
Luminescent dreams lead the way.

Falling Stars and Flickering Hopes

Stars descend like whispered wishes,
In the night, the heart reminisces.
Hopes like fireflies in the dark,
Guiding us with their soft spark.

Each falling star, a tale unfolds,
Secrets shared with the night so bold.
Flickering dreams dance in the air,
A symphony of joyful flare.

In the silence, we make our plea,
For the stars to set us free.
With each shimmer, we find our way,
Falling hopes that light the gray.

As dawn breaks, the dreams may fade,
But in our hearts, they are replayed.
Flickering hopes, forever near,
In the night sky, crystal clear.

Midsummer Night's Reverie

The moonlight dances on the grass,
Whispers of dreams begin to pass.
Fireflies twinkle, a gentle glow,
In this moment, time moves slow.

Scent of jasmine fills the air,
Laughter echoes everywhere.
Under stars, our secrets spill,
In the night, our hearts stand still.

The breeze hums soft, a lullaby,
Tales of wonder, low and high.
With every heartbeat, the night unfolds,
In the warmth of summer's hold.

As shadows wane and dawn draws near,
We'll cherish moments held so dear.
Midsummer's night, a fleeting bliss,
In a world where nothing's amiss.

Secrets of the Wandering Stars

In the vastness, stars delight,
Each a story in the night.
Whispers travel on the breeze,
Secrets held with such great ease.

They twinkle far, yet close they seem,
Guiding lost souls like a dream.
Each constellation, a tale to tell,
In the cosmos, we know them well.

Wanderers of the velvet sky,
With every blink, they seem to sigh.
Their paths entwined in cosmic dance,
In their glow, we take a chance.

Beneath their watchful, ancient gaze,
We find our hopes in twilight's haze.
The secrets of the stars ignite,
In our hearts, a flickering light.

Glowing Horizons and Silent Paths

As dawn awakens with a sigh,
The horizons glow, painting the sky.
Silent paths lead where dreams reside,
In the stillness, our hopes collide.

The golden light of morning breaks,
Softly touching the tranquil lakes.
Each step forward, a gentle grace,
In the quiet, we find our place.

Through fields of gold and whispers sweet,
On this journey, our hearts will meet.
With every turn, a surprise awaits,
In the embrace of open gates.

Glowing horizons, a brand new day,
Silent paths that guide our way.
In nature's arms, we find our peace,
In every breath, our spirits release.

Beneath the Starry Veil

Beneath the veil of twinkling lights,
We gather dreams on starry nights.
The cosmos hums a lullaby,
As galaxies drift and wander by.

In whispers soft, the night unfolds,
Ancient stories of the bold.
Each star a beacon, bright and clear,
In their glow, we shed each fear.

The universe speaks in silent threads,
Woven closely, where hope treads.
Under the vast and endless dome,
We find the way to call it home.

Beneath the starry, timeless veil,
In every breath, we gently sail.
Together in this cosmic dance,
We'll weave our fate, our hearts' romance.

A Passage to the Dreamworld

In whispered hues the shadows creep,
Where gentle spirits freely leap.
A doorway opens in the night,
To realms of wonder, pure delight.

The stars ignite the velvet sky,
As dreamers soar, their spirits fly.
Through misty paths where hopes entwine,
In every heartbeat, magic shines.

The silent call sings soft and low,
Each heartbeat's pulse, a sacred flow.
In twilight's grasp, we find our fate,
As dreams awaken, never late.

So take my hand, we're bound to roam,
Through lands of thought, we call our home.
In every dream, the world we weave,
In endless night, we shall believe.

Moonbeams and Wandering Souls

Beneath the moon's enchanting glow,
The wandering souls begin to flow.
With silver light upon their way,
They dance through night, not far from day.

Whispers cradled in the breeze,
Secrets stilled among the trees.
In shadows deep, their laughter fades,
A tapestry of twilight shades.

Through fields of dreams, they drift and twine,
As moonlit paths begin to shine.
Each footstep soft, a gentle trace,
In evening's calm, they find their place.

Together bound in mystic flight,
They chase the stars, embrace the night.
In moonbeams bright, they find their role,
Two wandering hearts, one restless soul.

Reflections in the Gloom

In shadows deep, where silence sighs,
Reflections dance with whispered lies.
The echoes of lost time resound,
In haunted halls of dreams unbound.

Each flicker of the candle's glow,
Unveils the past we wish to know.
With heavy hearts, we trace our steps,
Through murky thoughts and soul's missteps.

Yet in the gloom, a spark ignites,
A glimmer of forgotten lights.
In whispered hope, we find our way,
As dawn unveils the break of day.

So heed the call of shadowed seams,
In every loss, it's stitched with dreams.
For every tear that carves the night,
Leads to the dawn, a brand new light.

The Sway of the Evening Breeze

The evening breeze begins to play,
With tender sighs that softly sway.
It cradles leaves, a gentle dance,
And whispers secrets in romance.

Through twilight's veil, it roams the land,
A fleeting touch, a lover's hand.
It stirs the flowers, lifts their souls,
As nature's heart in rhythm rolls.

In every gust, a story told,
Of cherished dreams and hearts of gold.
With every rustle, every sound,
The world itself begins to round.

So let us linger, breathe the night,
With every breath, a spark of light.
In twilight's sway, with soft embrace,
We find our joy in nature's grace.

Midnight's Gentle Embrace

In the hush of night, stars gleam bright,
Whispers of dreams take their flight.
Beneath the silver glow we sway,
In midnight's arms, we'll gently stay.

The world fades away, just you and me,
Lost in this moment, so blissfully free.
Hearts intertwined, under the dark,
Embraced by shadows, igniting a spark.

Soft breezes carry secrets untold,
As the night wraps us in silk and gold.
Each breath a promise, we're destined to keep,
In the depths of slumber, together we leap.

With every heartbeat, time stands still,
In midnight's embrace, we drink our fill.
The stars are our witness, the moon our guide,
In this gentle haven, together we bide.

Trails of the Moonlit Whisper

Footsteps dance on a path so bright,
Guided by the kiss of soft moonlight.
Through the trees, the shadows play,
Echoes of whispers lead the way.

Beneath the night's veil, stories unfold,
Secrets of the heart, tenderly told.
With each gentle rustle, we draw near,
The magic of night dispels our fear.

Stars above twinkle, a celestial choir,
Filling the silence with soft desire.
Hand in hand, as we wander far,
Lost in a world where dreams are the stars.

Every step a memory, sweet and pure,
In moonlit whispers, our souls allure.
As dawn approaches, we pause, we sigh,
In trails of starlight, love will not die.

Chasing After Dusk

Fleeting moments in the waning light,
Chasing shadows as day turns to night.
Colors blend in a vivid hue,
Stealing glances, just me and you.

The horizon glimmers, a farewell glow,
In the soft embrace of twilight's flow.
With every heartbeat, we race the sun,
In the fleeting magic, we come undone.

Whispers of dusk beckon us near,
In the tender glow, there's nothing to fear.
Through the dusk we float, hand in hand,
In this rhapsody, perfectly planned.

As the stars awaken, we chase our dreams,
In midnight's arms, everything gleams.
With laughter and light, we find our way,
Chasing after dusk, come what may.

Silhouettes of the Fading Light

In the twilight's breath, shadows collide,
Silhouettes dance as day waves goodbye.
Colors fade softly, a canvas so grand,
In the twilight's grip, we take our stand.

The last rays linger, a gentle caress,
Wrapping us both in a soft, warm dress.
As night falls gently, our spirits soar,
In fading light, we yearn for more.

The universe hums a sweet serenade,
In silhouettes cast, our dreams are made.
With each passing moment, we grow entwined,
In the echoes of dusk, our hearts aligned.

Under the blanket of the night's embrace,
We linger longer, in this sacred space.
With shadows as witnesses, we softly ignite,
In silhouettes of the fading light.

Moonlit Paths of Wonder

Whispers dance upon the breeze,
As shadows weave through ancient trees.
The moon, a lantern in the night,
Guides our hearts, a soft delight.

Each step unveils a secret bright,
Where dreams and fears take gentle flight.
Through shimmering glow, we find our way,
In the stillness of the night's ballet.

Dreams Adrift on Celestial Winds

Stars above, a tapestry,
We ride the winds, both wild and free.
In night's embrace, we chase the glow,
Of dreams that drift like suns below.

With every whisper, fate entwines,
As hearts align with cosmic signs.
To sail through skies, a quest begun,
Where memories dance, and shadows run.

Starlit Journeys Beneath the Pines

Beneath the boughs, in twilight's gleam,
We wander softly, lost in dream.
The air is thick with secrets old,
As night unfolds her tales retold.

With starlight guiding every step,
In nature's arms, our souls adept.
We weave through paths of silver light,
Embarking on adventures bright.

Hushed Echoes of the Fading Light

As dusk descends and shadows play,
  The echoes of the day drift away.
  In quiet corners, whispers sigh,
    A lullaby beneath the sky.

With every moment, memories fade,
Yet in the stillness, dreams are made.
In twilight's glow, we seek the night,
  Where hopes reside in fading light.

Enigmas of the Nighttime Journey

Shadows dance in silent hues,
Whispers ride the velvet breeze,
Footsteps echo, softly muse,
Where will the winding pathway lead?

Stars above, like watchful eyes,
Guide the traveler, lost but bold,
Through the dark where mystery lies,
Stories of the night unfold.

Each corner holds a secret tight,
Wrapped in fog, a tale untold,
Paths converge under the moonlight,
In the dark, the heart grows old.

What awaits at journey's end?
Questions linger, dreams take flight,
With every turn, the echoes blend,
In the enigma of the night.

Moonlit Pathways and Starry Whispers

Glowing trails beneath the firmament,
Silver beams on rivers flow,
Step by step with firm intent,
Where the wild starlights grow.

Leaves rustle, secrets shared,
Voices murmur in delight,
In this sacred space, we dared,
To walk the paths of the night.

Moonlit shadows weave their tales,
Guiding hearts through darkened dreams,
On this journey, the spirit sails,
Lost in soft, celestial gleams.

Every star, a beacon near,
Mapping worlds of hope and grace,
As we wander without fear,
In this cosmic, timeless place.

Silhouetted Dreams of Dusk

The horizon blushes, night's embrace,
Silhouettes against the glow,
In shades of twilight, we find our place,
Where dreams and realities flow.

Flickering lights of the fading day,
Offer solace, gentle sighs,
In their warmth, shadows play,
As we hear the night's soft cries.

Each heartbeat echoes in the night,
As dusk wraps all in tender care,
Fleeting thoughts take graceful flight,
In the coolness of the air.

With the stars, our dreams ascend,
To whimsical heights we dare,
In these moments, we transcend,
Finding magic everywhere.

Enchanted Reflections at Sundown

Golden hues embrace the sky,
Whispers of the day take flight,
Water's mirror reflects our sigh,
In the calm of fading light.

Time stands still, an endless view,
As dusk slowly draws her lace,
Every wave, a story new,
Captured in the sunset's grace.

Voices of the evening call,
Softly blending with the tide,
In this magical, timeless hall,
Where day and night collide.

As the sun bows to the sea,
Promises made under shades of gold,
In these moments, we are free,
In the warmth of twilight's hold.

Starlit Dreams and Wandering Souls

Under skies of velvet hue,
Whispers of the night ensue.
Stars above, a guiding light,
For wandering souls taking flight.

Each dream spun in silver threads,
In the silence, hope embeds.
Through the dark, they softly glide,
On the breeze, they gently bide.

Time may flow like water clear,
Yet the heart, it draws us near.
To the realms where shadows play,
And starlit dreams hold sway.

In this dance of fate and chance,
Souls entwined in cosmic dance.
With every wish upon a star,
They wander forth, though near or far.

The Twilight of Innocence

In the glow of fading light,
Innocence takes flight from sight.
Shadows stretch upon the ground,
A whispered truth, a haunting sound.

Joy once danced in laughter's call,
But twilight casts a somber pall.
Childish dreams, now bittersweet,
In the dusk, they face defeat.

Yet in this twilight's gentle grace,
Memories find their rightful place.
The echoes of a time so pure,
Still linger, though they cannot endure.

Hold the moments, soft and dear,
For twilight's veil draws ever near.
In this haze of soft despair,
Innocence will linger there.

The Way of the Wandering Moon

Amidst the night, the moon does roam,
Her silver glow, a heart's true home.
Guiding tides and dreams anew,
Through every phase, she whispers too.

With craters deep like olden tales,
Her beauty dances, never pales.
In the silence, secrets bloom,
As shadows stretch beneath her plume.

Each journey taken, vast and wide,
The wandering moon, with grace, does glide.
Over valleys and mountains high,
A sentinel in the starry sky.

So let us wander in her light,
Chasing dreams into the night.
For in her glow, we find our way,
In the heart of night, we choose to stay.

Twilight Whispers and Forgotten Tales

In twilight's hush, old stories sigh,
From lips of legends drifting by.
Whispers weave through dusky air,
Forgotten tales, no longer bare.

Every shadow holds a spark,
Of dreams that bloomed within the dark.
Echoes of a time long past,
Flicker softly, still held fast.

With every breeze, a season's breath,
Recalls the joy and sorrows' depth.
In twilight's embrace, we find our place,
Among the whispers, we interlace.

So gather 'round and listen well,
As the night unfolds her spell.
For in this quiet, we unveil,
The magic of forgotten tales.

Reverie Beneath a Canopy of Stars

Underneath the vast, dark sky,
Stars like diamonds gently sigh.
A blanket soft, a world so still,
Whispers linger, hearts fulfill.

Moonlight dances on the earth,
Paints the night with silver birth.
Dreams unfurl, like leaves in spring,
In this night, my soul takes wing.

Each twinkle tells a tale of old,
Stories wrapped in gleaming gold.
Nature's lullaby softly plays,
In the silence of starry days.

Time stands still, the night is deep,
Within this dream, the world will sleep.
Beneath the stars, I find my peace,
In this reverie, my fears release.

The Twilight Sojourn

A gentle dusk begins to fade,
Brushes skies in purple shade.
Shadows stretch as colors blend,
The day's light finds its slow end.

Footsteps echo on the trail,
Nature sings a sweet, soft wail.
Trees whisper secrets to the night,
In twilight's glow, all feels right.

Stars awake in twilight's grace,
Each one shines, a timeless face.
A journey starts with heart aglow,
In the quiet, spirits flow.

As the sun succumbs to rest,
Nighttime wraps the world in zest.
Wander on through silver beams,
In twilight's arms, weave your dreams.

Whispers of the Evening Breeze

Softly comes the evening breeze,
Caressing leaves on swaying trees.
A murmur flows through fields of grain,
Nature's breath, a sweet refrain.

Stars emerge in shimmering light,
Guiding dreams into the night.
Silhouettes dance on shadows cast,
In the calm, our hearts beat fast.

Moonlight spills like silver threads,
Weaving soft paths where magic treads.
Whispers float, the night is near,
Every sigh, a wish sincere.

Let the breeze carry your prayer,
In this twilight, love is rare.
Close your eyes, feel the embrace,
In the night, find your pace.

Celestial Pathways to Fantasy

On celestial pathways, we glide,
Stars as guides, in dreams we ride.
Galaxies swirl in cosmic dance,
In starlit realms, we find our chance.

Nebulas bloom in colors bright,
Painting wonders in the night.
Each twinkle whispers tales untold,
Of far-off worlds, and treasures bold.

Floating high on dreams so grand,
Exploring realms of distant land.
The universe sings, a symphony,
In this magic, we're set free.

Through the cosmos, hand in hand,
We'll chart our course, a daring plan.
With every star, our hearts expand,
In this fantasy, forever stand.

Silhouettes in the Gathering Shade

In twilight's embrace we find our way,
Figures dance where whispers play.
Trees stand tall, their secrets worn,
Silhouettes in shadows, dreams reborn.

Softly beneath the canopy's sigh,
Echoes linger, a gentle high.
Footsteps hush, the night draws near,
In the gathering shade, all becomes clear.

Night blooms softly, stars ignite,
Guiding us through a velvet night.
Each shape tells tales of love and grace,
In the tangled light, we find our place.

Together we linger, lost in the dream,
In silhouettes' dance, we become a team.
The whispers fade, but the bond remains,
In the gathering shade, our spirit gains.

Nocturnal Tales of Resting Hearts

In hallowed night where shadows creep,
We share our dreams, our secrets deep.
Resting hearts in quietude,
Nocturnal tales in solitude.

The moonlight weaves its silver thread,
Over secrets softly said.
Each sigh a melody in the dark,
Igniting hope, a fleeting spark.

Branches sway with the gentle breeze,
While nightingales sing beneath the trees.
Whispers of hearts that learn to mend,
In night's embrace, the lost will tend.

Soft starlight kisses weary eyes,
In dreams we chase the endless skies.
Together we breathe, our spirits soar,
Nocturnal tales forever more.

A Dance of Shadows and Secrets

In moonlit whispers, shadows sway,
A dance unfolds where secrets lay.
Veils of darkness as partners glide,
In the night's embrace, we confide.

Footsteps echo on cobblestone,
A melody shared, yet felt alone.
Each shadow dances, each secret unfolds,
In the twilight's charm, magic holds.

Veils of silence, soft and wide,
With every twirl, we let fear slide.
The world unseen, where dreams ignite,
A dance of shadows, pure delight.

In this realm where hearts combine,
With every turn, our spirits align.
Secrets whispered through moonlit streams,
A dance forever, lost in dreams.

The Quietude of Dusk's Caress

At dusk's arrival, silence reigns,
A tender brush of soothing refrains.
Colors fade in the softest light,
The quietude settles, calm and bright.

Hushed are the sounds of the late-day sighs,
As day retreats and the night complies.
Beneath the canopy, peace unfurls,
In dusk's caress, the world swirls.

The fading horizon blushes gold,
A promise whispered, gently told.
In the stillness, hearts unite,
Finding solace as night takes flight.

In the cradle of dusk, we find our grace,
A moment caught in time and space.
With every breath, the night we embrace,
In the quietude of dusk's soft place.

Fantasies Woven in Gossamer Gleam

In twilight's hush, dreams softly sway,
Glimmers of hope in the fading day.
Whispers of magic in the starlit air,
Woven with wishes, delicate and rare.

A tapestry rich, spun from light,
Each thread a story, bathed in night.
Laughter and love in a soft embrace,
Fantasies danced in a dreamy space.

Unravel the secrets the shadows keep,
Enchanting visions that drift to sleep.
Across the horizon, colors blend,
Gossamer dreams that never end.

Enchanted Hours of the Dusk's Serenade

The sun bows gracefully, a golden crown,
As shadows lengthen, and day slips down.
Crickets begin their twilight song,
In the dusk's embrace, where hearts belong.

Mellow tones of purple blend with rose,
As cool breezes whisper through the throes.
Stars awaken, twinkling bright,
A serenade lingers in the night.

Lost in the moment where time stands still,
The world draws close, with a gentle thrill.
Enchanting hours wrapped in night's shawl,
Together we rise, together we fall.

Soft Glimmers in the Penumbra

In the penumbra, shadows tease,
Soft glimmers dance with a tranquil ease.
A world aglow with silken grace,
Where light and darkness weave a lace.

Flickering whispers in the twilight air,
Echoing secrets that spirits share.
Each sigh of night, a gentle muse,
Softly along the horizon, we cruise.

The moon's embrace, a silver light,
Guides us through the velvety night.
With every heartbeat, the silence beams,
In the penumbra, we weave our dreams.

The Wilderness of Lullabies

In the wilderness, where shadows play,
Lullabies echo at the close of day.
Trees sway softly, a soothing embrace,
Nature's rhythm, a calming space.

Crickets serenade the fading light,
As stars awaken to paint the night.
Whispers of breezes, soft and low,
Guide weary hearts to their restful flow.

Through fields of dreams, where memories lie,
The wild serenades with a gentle sigh.
In this sacred realm, we drift and rest,
The wilderness cradles us, truly blessed.

Embracing the Quietude of Night

In shadows deep, the whispers breathe,
A tranquil hush, where thoughts can weave.
The moon, a guide in ink-black skies,
Invites the stars, like dreams, to rise.

Crickets sing a lullaby near,
The world slows down, the heart draws near.
With every sigh, the night unfolds,
Secrets kept, and stories told.

Embrace the stillness, let it flow,
The night holds peace in its soft glow.
A canvas vast, where spirits dance,
In quietude, find your chance.

So close your eyes, and drift away,
In the night's embrace, let worries stay.
For in this calm, find strength anew,
In the silent depths of night's cool hue.

Fables in the Starlight

Underneath the vast expanse,
Stories twinkle, take a chance.
Each star a tale, a dream that gleams,
Whispered softly, hint of schemes.

The night unfolds its ancient lore,
With every sparkle, hearts explore.
Once upon a time, they say,
In starlit realms, the shadows play.

Adventures born in moonlit glow,
Where wishes fly, and hopes will grow.
Fables woven through the sky,
In dreamy paths, let spirits fly.

So listen close to night's sweet song,
The universe where we belong.
In starlight's embrace, dreams ignite,
And carve our fables in the night.

Roots of the Evening Breeze

The evening breeze begins to weave,
Through trembling leaves, a gentle reprieve.
It wraps around with whispers low,
And all the world begins to slow.

The roots of dusk stretch wide and deep,
Awakening secrets from their sleep.
Crickets chirp, a rhythmic sound,
In twilight's grip, beauty is found.

A dance of shadows, soft and light,
The earth unrolls in waning night.
With every sigh, the air does tell,
Of dreams that rise and thoughts that swell.

So breathe in deep the evening air,
Feel the roots of calm everywhere.
Let worries drift like clouds above,
In the gentle breeze, find your love.

The Storyteller's Dusk

As daylight fades, a tale does start,
In whispers soft, it warms the heart.
The storyteller finds his place,
In twilight's glow, a sacred space.

With every word, a magic spun,
From ancient times, when day was done.
He paints with voice, the stars aligned,
In dusk, the threads of fate entwined.

Listen close, as tales unfold,
Of heroes brave and hearts of gold.
In shadows deep, the stories bloom,
Illuminated from the gloom.

The night, a canvas, vast and wide,
Invites each soul to take a ride.
In tales of yore, we find our way,
The storyteller's dusk brings light to gray.

Navigating the Nebulous Night

In shadows deep where whispers dwell,
The stars align, their secrets swell.
A path unwinds through cosmic sight,
Dancing dreams take flight in night.

With every breath, the silence grows,
As twilight wraps like gentle prose.
Soft echoes trace the moonlit way,
A song of dusk begins to play.

Through veils of mist, my heart does steer,
In search of tales the darkness hears.
The cosmos gleams with tales untold,
In whispered winds, the night unfolds.

Each step I take, a chance I find,
In nebulous realms, my spirit blind.
Yet in the vast, I find my light,
Forever bound to the starry night.

The Color of Dusk

In hues of lavender, day does wane,
With whispered sighs, the night remains.
The sky blushes in amber light,
As shadows bloom, embracing night.

The world transforms, a canvas bright,
With strokes of gold, then soft twilight.
Dusk's gentle brush creates a scene,
A fleeting kiss, tranquil and keen.

Each moment glows as time slips by,
In vibrant whispers, the colors sigh.
The edge of day, a dreamer's touch,
In every shade, we feel so much.

Like fleeting hours, the day does fall,
Yet in its warmth, we sense it all.
For in the color of dusk's embrace,
We find our peace, our sacred space.

Farewell to the Dimming Light

The dusk descends with gentle grace,
Whispers fade in twilight's embrace.
Stars awaken, soft and bright,
Yet I bid farewell to the dimming light.

Shadows creep with silent sighs,
As day retreats, the night replies.
Memories linger in the night air,
For moments lost, I pause and care.

A world unseen but ever near,
In echoes of laughter, I hold dear.
The horizon swallows the sun's last fight,
A silent promise in the fading light.

So here I stand, with heart set free,
Embracing the night, my soul in glee.
With every star that takes its flight,
I find my peace in the dimming light.

The Draw of the Starlit Road

Beneath the sky where whispers gleam,
I walk the path of a silver dream.
Each step a dance with fate's embrace,
The starlit road, my chosen place.

The night unfolds its velvet gown,
As twinkling lights draw me down.
Every shadow holds a story untold,
In the heart of darkness, the brave grow bold.

With every breath, the world stands still,
The moonlight guides with gentle will.
In night's embrace, I lose my load,
A wanderer's heart on the starlit road.

So let me wander, let me roam,
In the night's embrace, I find my home.
For every star and whispered ode,
Leads me onward down the starlit road.

Milton Keynes UK
Ingram Content Group UK Ltd.
UKHW020635301124
451843UK00006B/122